KICK, JUMP, CHEER!

CHEERLEADING CAMP

BY SARA GREEN

BELLWETHER MEDIA • MINNEAPOLIS, MN

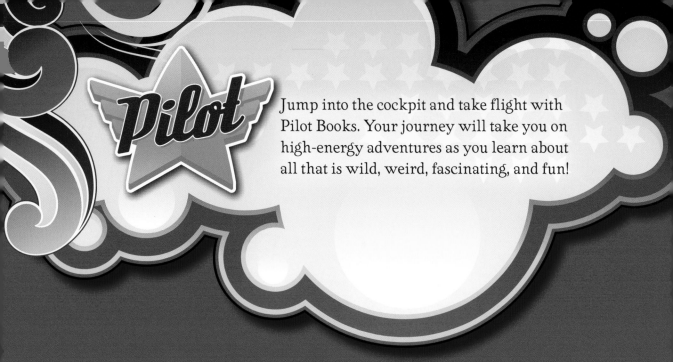

Jump into the cockpit and take flight with Pilot Books. Your journey will take you on high-energy adventures as you learn about all that is wild, weird, fascinating, and fun!

This edition first published in 2012 by Bellwether Media, Inc.

No part of this publication may be reproduced in whole or in part without written permission of the publisher.
For information regarding permission, write to Bellwether Media, Inc., Attention: Permissions Department,
5357 Penn Avenue South, Minneapolis, MN 55419.

Library of Congress Cataloging-in-Publication Data
Green, Sara, 1964–
 Cheerleading camp / by Sara Green.
    p. cm. — (Pilot books: kick, jump, cheer!)
 Includes bibliographical references and index.
 Summary: "Engaging images accompany information about cheerleading camp. The combination of high-interest subject matter and narrative text is intended for students in grades 3 through 7"—Provided by publisher.
 ISBN 978-1-60014-647-3 (hardcover : alk. paper)
 1. Cheerleading—Juvenile literature. I. Title.
 LB3635.G742 2011
 791.6'4—dc22   2011010379

Printed in the United States of America, North Mankato, MN.

080111   1187

CONTENTS

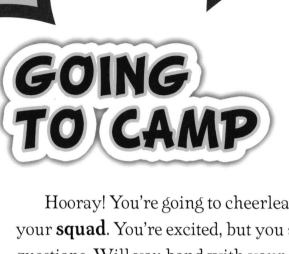

GOING TO CAMP

Hooray! You're going to cheerleading camp with your **squad**. You're excited, but you also have many questions. Will you bond with your squad? What will the camp instructors be like? Will the skills be difficult to learn? Don't worry! You're going to have a great time. There are many reasons to go to cheerleading camp. You will form strong bonds with members of your squad, learn new skills, and gain confidence. You will also have a lot of fun!

THE HISTORY OF CHEERLEADING CAMP

Cheerleading camps have been around for over 50 years. Lawrence Herkimer, also known as Herkie, started the first camp in 1948. It took place at Sam Houston State University in Huntsville, Texas. One boy and 52 girls attended the camp. Herkie did **routines** with **tumbling** to show how exciting cheerleading could be. Instructors taught campers how to create rhymes and speak with confidence. The next year, Herkie drew 350 cheerleaders to his camp. Cheerleading camps soon began to appear throughout the United States. Today, thousands of campers attend camps each summer.

Herkimer invented a jump that is still popular today. To perform a "Herkie," kick one leg straight out to the side and bend the other leg so your knee faces the ground.

Lawrence "Herkie" Herkimer

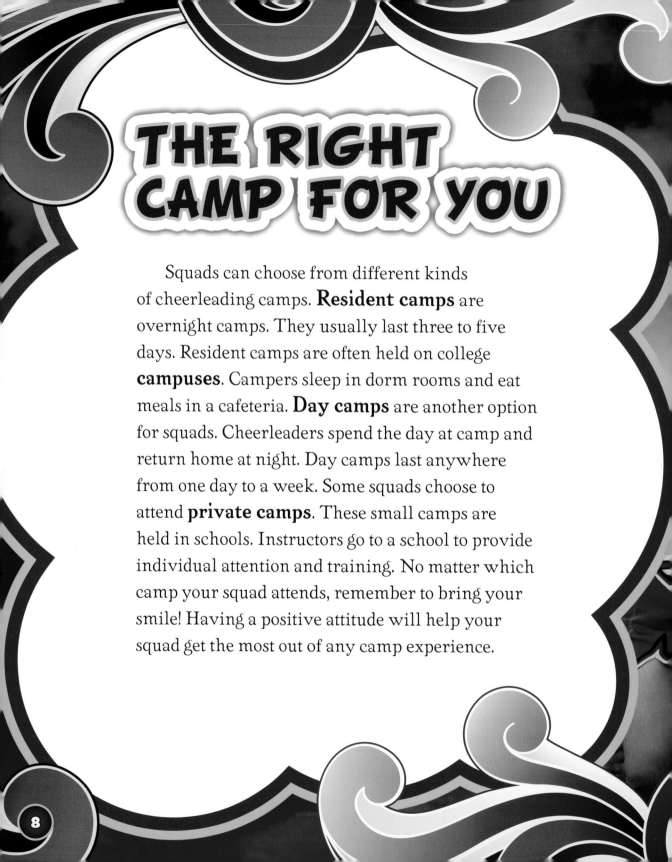

THE RIGHT CAMP FOR YOU

Squads can choose from different kinds of cheerleading camps. **Resident camps** are overnight camps. They usually last three to five days. Resident camps are often held on college **campuses**. Campers sleep in dorm rooms and eat meals in a cafeteria. **Day camps** are another option for squads. Cheerleaders spend the day at camp and return home at night. Day camps last anywhere from one day to a week. Some squads choose to attend **private camps**. These small camps are held in schools. Instructors go to a school to provide individual attention and training. No matter which camp your squad attends, remember to bring your smile! Having a positive attitude will help your squad get the most out of any camp experience.

If you go to a resident camp, remember to bring decorations. Some squads like to have decoration competitions. Cheerleaders decorate their doors or rooms based on the contest theme.

TRUST MAKES A TEAM

It is very important that cheerleaders on a squad trust each other. If there are new members on your squad, spend time getting to know each other before camp. Have a sleepover, go to the movies, or throw a pizza party. Your squad will have a better time at camp if all the cheerleaders feel like they belong to the group.

Don't worry if you aren't part of a school squad. You can still go to a resident camp or day camp. The instructors will match you up with other cheerleaders just like you!

When you leave for camp, remember to bring matching uniforms and hair accessories. They will help you feel like a team and help others identify your squad. At camp, set aside any personal problems you may have with someone. Camp is the time to focus on team spirit. If problems come up, calmly talk them over with the squad. You avoid conflict when you solve problems as a group.

LEARNING SKILLS AND HAVING FUN

Being in shape will help you get the most out of cheerleading camp. You want to feel healthy and energetic instead of tired and sore. Your coach can help you build strength, **stamina**, and **flexibility** before camp. You can run, bike, or swim to build stamina. Push-ups and sit-ups will help you build strength. Remember to stretch your muscles every day. This will keep them loose and prevent injuries.

Don't forget about your voice! It is one of your most important cheerleading tools. You want to keep your voice strong and clear. Your coach can teach you how to do this. Shouting from your chest instead of your throat helps you project your voice without straining it. Lowering your **pitch** helps you yell loudly without screeching.

Expect to stay busy with activities and classes at camp. Instructors will help you master old skills and learn new ones. They will teach you new **cheers**, dances, jumps, and **stunts**. Your squad will get tips on how to encourage crowds and raise school spirit at **pep rallies**. You will also do team-building exercises. These activities help squad members form tighter bonds with each other. For example, your squad might create an original cheer that shows off everyone's skills and spirit!

The instructors help make camp fun and challenging. Many are former high school, college, or professional cheerleaders. They know what it takes to be a top cheerleader. Good instructors always put safety first. You should never perform skills that you are not ready to do. With the help of talented instructors, your squad will improve and grow as a team.

Most camps schedule free time for other activities. You might take a swim, go bowling, or relax with your squad. Some camps plan fun evening activities such as ice cream socials, movies, or even talent shows!

ALL-AMERICAN TRYOUT

One of the most exciting parts of cheerleading camp is the All-American **tryout**. All-American cheerleaders are selected from the thousands of campers who try out each summer. About 1 in 10 cheerleaders is chosen. It is a big honor to be named an All-American cheerleader. Judges look at cheering skills, athletic ability, and leadership qualities. They also pay close attention to character. Is the cheerleader a team player? Does the cheerleader treat others with respect and kindness? Attitude is just as important as skills and abilities.

All-American cheerleaders receive a medal, a patch, and a certificate. They also have the chance to travel. They cheer in parades, festivals, and large sporting events. If this sounds like something you would enjoy, be sure to enter the All-American tryout at camp!

CAMP AWARDS

Awards are another fun part of cheerleading camp. Instructors give out daily awards to individual cheerleaders and squads for their hard work. At the end of each day, instructors award a **spirit stick** to the squad with the most spirit. Squads often decorate their sticks with team colors. Sometimes they attach bells and other noisemakers to them. Each team tries to win as many spirit sticks as possible!

On the last day of camp, friends and family are invited to a special awards ceremony. Squads perform routines that show off their new skills. Instructors give final awards. Squads with the best leadership, **sportsmanship**, and technical skills win trophies. The most improved squad also wins an award.

BRINGING CAMP CHEER HOME

Your time at camp will go quickly, but the memories will stay with you forever. Cheerleading camp is about bonding with teammates, improving skills, learning new routines, and having fun. You will grow as an individual and as a squad. Maybe you or someone on your squad will make the All-American team! If your squad wins a spirit stick, use it to encourage team spirit at your first home game.

After camp, you'll be more enthusiastic than ever about cheering with your squad. You will bring home great ideas for planning pep rallies and boosting school spirit. The skill, confidence, and spirit you gain from camp will catch every fan's eye!

GLOSSARY

campuses—the buildings and grounds of colleges or universities

cheers—long phrases yelled during breaks in play; jumps and stunts often go along with cheers.

day camps—camps held during the day; day camps usually last one to five days.

flexibility—the ability to stretch and move the body with ease

pep rallies—gatherings held before sporting events to boost school spirit and encourage sports teams

pitch—the highness or lowness of the voice

private camps—camps held in the privacy of a squad's school; cheerleaders receive one-on-one instruction from camp staff.

resident camps—overnight camps that usually last three to five days

routines—sequences of moves that cheerleaders practice and perform

spirit stick—an award given to the squad that shows the most spirit; cheerleaders use them to boost school spirit.

sportsmanship—showing fair play, respect for others, and grace whether winning or losing

squad—a group of cheerleaders that works together as a team

stamina—the ability to do something for a long time

stunts—cheerleading moves that involve climbing and lifting; in some stunts cheerleaders are thrown into the air.

tryout—an event where people perform skills for coaches or judges in order to make a team

tumbling—gymnastics skills such as cartwheels and handsprings; many cheerleading squads use tumbling in their routines.

TO LEARN MORE

At the Library

Crossingham, John. *Cheerleading in Action*. New York, N.Y.: Crabtree Pub. Co., 2003.

Gruber, Beth. *Cheerleading for Fun.* Minneapolis, Minn.: Compass Point Books, 2004.

Rusconi, Ellen. *Cheerleading.* New York, N.Y.: Children's Press, 2001.

On the Web

Learning more about cheerleading is as easy as 1, 2, 3.

1. Go to www.factsurfer.com.

2. Enter "cheerleading" into the search box.

3. Click the "Surf" button and you will see a list of related Web sites.

With factsurfer.com, finding more information is just a click away.

INDEX

The images in this book are reproduced through the courtesy of: Juan Martinez, front cover; Shane Martin/Bucs Cheerleading, p. 4; Digital Vision/Getty Images, p. 5; Alin Dragulin/Photolibrary, p. 7 (top); National Cheerleaders Association, p. 7 (bottom); Image Source/Getty Images, pp. 9, 19; Jim Cayer/Cayer's Sports Action Photography, pp. 10-11, 13, 15, 20-21; Alan Edwards/Alamy, p. 16.